ACTION:

The catalyst to achieve all your dreams and more!

By Kris Patterson

Kris Patterson. Action: The catalyst to achieve all your dreams and more.

ISBN: 978-0-9881204-3-3
ISBN eBook: 978-0-9881204-8-8

I dedicate this book to all of the people who are on the cusp of becoming. I hope this is the push you need.

Kris

TABLE OF CONTENTS

ntroduction ix
Why I wrote this book 1
Transforming Power 5
Gratitude 9
Goal Setting 11
101 Questions 13
Communication 19
Relationships 21
Grief, Loss and Hope 23
Forgiveness 27
Financial 29
Fear 31
Worry 33
Regret 35
Persistence 37
Life Long Learning 39
Discipline 41
Time Management 43
Productivity 45
Hoarder and Clutter 49
Action Habits for Success 51
A Paradox of Time 59
Conclusion 61
Acknowledgements 62
Resources 63
Supplemental Appendix 66
Seven Disciplines for Success 66
Seven Rules for the 21st Century 66
10 steps to Stop Procrastinating 66
9 steps to Problem Solving 66
10 Questions for Establishing Rapport 67
7 Success Principals 67
Affirmations for building Self Esteem 67
12 Things to Remember 68
Advice for Life 68
Advice for Coping with Anxiety that is 300 years old. 69

The credit belongs to the man who is actually in the arena, whose face is marred by dust, sweat, and blood, who knows the greatest enthusiasms, the great devotions, and spends himself in a worthy cause; who at best, if he wins, knows the thrills of high achievement, and if he fails, at least fails daring greatly, so that his place shall never be with those cold and timid souls who knew neither victory nor defeat.

Theodore Roosevelt

INTRODUCTION

"The best thing to do is the right thing, the second best thing to do is the wrong thing. The worst thing to do is nothing." – Teddy Roosevelt.

It takes only one idea to change your life. For me it was the realization that action was essential to happiness. The message of this book is very simple, **TAKE ACTION**. Nothing really happens until you start taking action. You can have all kinds of great ideas and thoughts but nothing will ever materialize until you begin to do something. I wanted to keep the core concept of this book simple. The important part is to take action of some kind and I wanted to provide some directions for you to proceed once you have decided on the importance of taking action. Along with some of the lessons I have learned, I've also provided some information and resources that will allow you to improve your life in areas that will directly contribute to your success and happiness including financial, time management and relationships as well as other success tips.

WHY I WROTE THIS BOOK

"When you are inspired by some great purpose, some extraordinary project, all your thoughts break their bonds, your mind transcends limitations, your consciousness expands in every direction and you find yourself in a new, great and wonderful world. Dormant forces, faculties and talents become alive and you discover yourself to be a greater person than you ever dreamed yourself to be." – Patanjali

I have heard it said that people don't care how much you know until, they know how much you care so i wanted to talk about some the reasons why I wrote this book. I had a few years where all I wanted to do was get through the day. It all began when I lost my daughter, then a severe health scare with a ruptured appendix and two car accidents as well a tremendous amount of relationship drama. All I felt like doing was running away which I did for a few years. I kept going and going, somewhere hoping deep down that the next day would bring something different. I was so sick of the life I was leading, I would retch because of it. A relationship I was in ended and despite how painful it was, it would be the wake-up call I needed and with the loss of both my mom and dad only eight months apart everything was catching up to me. Somehow I knew there was supposed to be some meaning in life so I'd always been reading, studying and searching.

It was all great information and allowed me to help people during the four years I spent doing crisis intervention work. I was never able to get what I wanted from this study because I was missing the critical factor of action and application. In September 2011 I made a decision that I could no longer tolerate my life as it was. So I resolved to change it. I looked at several areas: financial, relationship, etc. I had been holding onto a lot of anger and resentment over the loss of my daughter and I decided to let it go. I undertook a painful process to produce a book chronicling her life, and the lessons I learned from that experience. This allowed me to let go of some of the pain as well as help other people with their own grief and raise funds for an organization the compassionate friends. It felt good to transform a negative experience into a positive effect for people. Transformative power is a concept I was introduced to in a workshop called the alternatives to violence program.

I've always felt that there was more to life. I've read thousands of books looking for something. I am not sure what I was even looking for. I assumed I was incomplete in some way and tried to compensate for this by acquiring knowledge. I did learn many things and acquired much trivial information. It was years later, triggered by a period of terrible events, that I began searching deeper. I was working at a job which although skilled at, I hated. I met a woman who I had a child with which we lost. Three months after that my appendix ruptured. A month after that I was in a car accident. After physiotherapy and rehabilitation, a year later there was a second car accident. This left me with pain which will be a part of me for the rest of my life. I felt like life was one constant crisis and I had lost hope that things would ever change. I finally met a great woman who I thought I would spend the rest of my life with. Things returned to mostly calm and I thought happiness loomed.

I changed jobs and begun to rebuild my life. Three years later my mother was diagnosed with pancreatic cancer and was only given a maximum of six months to live. I moved back home to help her. Eight months after my mom succumbed to cancer, I was unsuccessfully applying CPR to my father the day before my 35th birthday. I think he died from a broken heart. I was thoroughly burnt out. I was forced to act as an executor for both of my parents simultaneously. This period of time lead me to reflect upon my life and I did not like what I saw. I had gone from one problem to another just reacting. I decided that I couldn't live like this anymore. I made the decision to change right then and there and rock bottom became the solid foundation on which I rebuilt my life.

The first step was deciding. To decide derives from Latin meaning to cut off from. Once you decide you are going to do something and you cut yourself off from any other choice it is amazing what you can accomplish. Although the decision to change was made quickly, I had many setbacks before I finally began to put it all together, but it definitely all began with action.

I was always close to my parents and they helped make me the person I am today. My dad's passing was the turning point in my life. Before things settled down my relationship had also ended, this was the final step on the journey I was going through at that time. I took the time to analyze how I got to where I was and how to change things to get what I wanted. I also figured out where I wanted to go. I took action and I completed several courses of things I was interested in for some time. I had spent tens of thousands of dollars on audio programs from Nightingale Conant and had never taken the time to listen to them and absorb the knowledge that was offered.

I immediately began rectifying this. I spent hours every day reading, studying, working, writing and changing myself. This book is the representation of some of these insights as well as some practical strategies to improve your life, and create the life you were meant to live.

I did have the advantage of having some good habits already. I've always enjoyed reading, studying and looking for ways of self-improvement. I started by spending a few hours along with a notebook dreaming and picturing what my ideal life looked like. I listed all of my goals. I included goals in different life areas like physical goals, charity goals, educational goals and item goals. For example, in what kind of house do I want to live in? Where did I want to live? etc. Once the decision was made I started stripping away anything in my life that was not in line with how I wanted my life to be.

During the time of the loss of my parents, I also lost a woman I loved very much. She was the woman I thought I would spend the rest of my life with. She felt like I wasn't open to her with my feelings. The reality was that I was overwhelmed with everything else going on. I should have told her how I felt but there was so much going on I was just trying to keep my head above water. I took a lot of time to analyze this relationship and what had gone wrong. I think that is important to not shut down emotionally. I was told the worst part for her was that I was pushing her away. I was not conscious of doing this but I think it was a protective measure for me because my life had underwent so many changes I was telling everybody to leave so I could protect myself from any more loss by controlling when they left. The loss of this relationship forced me deeper into myself and was the final catalyst for me to redesign my life, implementing the steps which are included in this book. You can learn from your mistakes and even better you can learn from other people's mistakes. I certainly hope that this book isn't calling to you because of these types of losses but I want you to know that there is always hope. Change is a constant in life and by taking the right action at the right time we are able to be the best people we are able to be.

My life really took off when I implemented these strategies into my daily life. My life became immeasurably better once I began applying the information I had spent years learning. Once I decided to change opportunities came up again and again. I completely analyzed my life and thought about what got me to this point and where did I want to go from here. It was a remarkably draining process. My life in its entirety changed due to zero-based thinking. This is a management concept where you ask yourself "knowing everything you know now would you still enter into" a job for example if the answer is no your next question should be how do I get out of this as fast as possible. I applied this philosophy to every area of my life.

In the past I have chosen activities which went along with my limitations self-imposed or not. "Someday", "One of these days" and "should" must be removed from your vocabulary as they really hold you back from everything in life that you could be experiencing. I had to learn this lesson over and over again. From then on I did something to de-clutter my life spiritually, physically, or mentally and it led to a lot of positive changes in my life in all areas. I was able to relinquish the strangle hold a lot of things had on my life such as grief and pain. I was unaware that they were having such a profound effect on my life until I cast them off. Action was the critical determinant. I wrote a pledge to myself and dated it and signed it. My life was transformed from that day forward.

You are where you are and what you are because of yourself. Everything you are today or ever will be in the future is up to you. Your life today is the sum total of your choices, decisions and actions up to this point. You can create your own future by changing your behaviors, you can change make new choices and decisions that are more consistent with the person you want to be and the things you want to accomplish with your life.

The problem with most self-help books is that they lead you to believe that there's something wrong or deficient with you. I want to give you the opposite message. I know you are all worthwhile just as you are. Everyone has a special message that they can share. I just want offer some tips to help you accomplish even more.

TRANSFORMING POWER

I had a revelation that I didn't like the way my life was going and that I was 100% responsible for it. I not only wanted to put my past behind me I wanted to transcend it. I looked at the areas which were most limiting me and I thought of ways to do good with some of the negative things that have happened in my life. I took this concept of transformative power and was able to help others through my own pain. In April 2010 I was told my mom had advanced pancreatic cancer and only had six months to live. I moved back home to help take care of her. This was a very tough time on me as I had to see a person I respected very much in a tremendous amount of pain while being able to do nothing to lessen it. My mom died on September 14, 2010. She was able to stay at home up until the last week. This coincided with something she wanted to get done. She lived her life for her family and for her work. She worked the entire time to make sure everybody had a note or card for their birthday or anniversary and Christmas presents. She did all of her Christmas shopping in June because she knew she would not be there. Eight months later on May 1, 2011 my dad passed away. I think he loved my mother so much that he couldn't stand to be apart from her. My dad was a local columnist writing a column on the history of our community. I needed a project to keep myself busy. I was going through a lot of feelings as well as going through his info to finish things off as an executor. I had been continuously told how many people looked forward to his columns and how missed it was. I decided to edit some of his columns into a book format and have it published. This turned out to be a way bigger task than I expected or was prepared for.

It was always my father's dream to have his columns published in a book format I was pleased to be able to complete his dream. I officially launched the book on August 30, 2012. I found the book helpful for myself and the community showed me overwhelming support and encouragement and they looked forward to it so much, that I prepared and published a second volume which was released May 16, 2013. The projects were done as a fundraiser for the museum and the archives. I don't always recommend a specific action for your grief but keeping busy can be in and of itself healing, I know it was for me.

Here is a photo from the signing at the first book launch.

Dragonfly Youth Project. 1999-2000. This was one of the best projects I was ever involved in. It taught me a lot about myself

This is from the second book launch.

It was a lot of work due to being an executor for both my mom and dad and working more than full-time It took a massive amount of action to accomplish but I think I will look back on it with pride.

I also think my dad would be flattered that people are still talking about his work after he was gone. I donated the proceeds to the museum and the archives of my hometown. This was a place that my dad was always going to, to do research. I am proud to have honored both my father and my community.

Transformative power which is taking something negative and transforming it into something positive represents a philosophy which has become an integral part of my life. I also applied this philosophy to loss of my daughter. I undertook a full review of my feelings, everything that I had spent years ignoring and repressing. I brought it all to the surface. I wrote a book about my experiences. Partly it was to help me with what I've been dragging around with me, but I also wanted to let people know it is okay to ask for and to receive help. I also wanted to raise awareness for the compassionate friends organization. This is a group of people who have lost a child and are offering support to others who

had experienced this loss. I feel like my healing never really started until I took action and began doing something about the grief and hurt I was feeling. When I wrote this book I experienced firsthand the healing power of taking action.

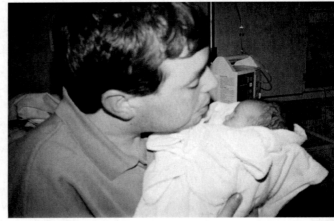

Ella and I

ACTION: *The Catalyst to Achieve All Your Dreams and More*

Eight years after the loss of my daughter I published "I will always love you Ella" "A story of loss and healing". I've had countless people come up to me to express how much the book has helped them. Many people have also experienced the loss of a child and were unable to talk about it and my book became a catalyst for them to start their own journey of healing. I'm very proud to have played a small role in that. The process of creating and publishing that book also improved my life as I was able to let go of a lot of pain and destructive emotions that had been ruling my life up till that point. Taking action and dealing with these feelings produced something that has been able to offer some relief for people. This was completely the result of action.

It's funny how life always teaches you exactly what you need to know when you need to know it. I've been blessed by some of the experiences I have had. Although I was not always happy at the time I have been able to help people in various capacities one of which was contributing more than 1500 volunteer hours on a crisis line. I have worked with people in all of my jobs and I consider myself very fortunate for the incredible people I've met and the lessons they taught me. I did pass through a period of darkness where I was lucky to have made it through. This period was a direct result of me not being in control of myself and my future. Once I took full responsibility my life began to take shape.

GRATITUDE

"Cultivate the habit of being grateful for every good thing that comes to you, and to give thanks continuously. And because all things have contributed to your advancement, you should include all things in your gratitude." – Ralph Waldo Emerson

One of the greatest tools that can change your life is that of gratitude. I made rapid progress in my life when I decided to embrace gratitude. I spent a lot of my life being angry and resentful. I've always done my best to be a cheerful person but it was time to take it to the next level. I also embraced charity and have been able to accomplish my goal of helping people through my donations to the Children's Hospital and to other causes such as our local literacy organization.

In 2004 I was in a car accident which required me to go through rehabilitation. I was well on my way to becoming better, approaching my full strength when approximately a year later I was involved in a second car accident. This accident left me with several injuries which linger to this day.

It took a lot of changing my mindset to get past the chronic pain. For me there is nothing worse than having something forced upon you and being able to do nothing about it. I spent some time feeling sorry for myself rather than getting on with my life. When the pain gets incredibly bad, I choose to reframe the experience and remember something positive about that day. I was on my way to work and I just had twins six weeks prior to this accident. They should have been in the car with me, but my mom kept them with her. The accident happened five blocks from my home and I always remind myself of how things could have been worse. This reframing reminds me of how precious and important life is. I also realized that you have a choice on what you choose to focus on. If you make the pain a part of yourself you can learn to transcend it.

My life really started to change when I embraced gratitude. I started to focus on what I have in my life rather than what I didn't have. Before I go to bed every day I think about a few things that I'm truly grateful for.

Ask yourself every day what three things you are grateful for, 20 ways to improve your job and thoughts for projects for the future

Children's Hospital Donation

Steve and Barb Kalugin are the Co-Chairs for the Port Alberni chapter of the Community for Kids program through BC Children's Hospital Foundation. The Community for Kids program participates in several initiatives throughout the year such as Jeans Day and the Festival of Trees. The Kalugins have brought their passion and knowledge to this position for more than twenty years.

This donation will be used to purchase a new ECG Heart Monitor. They are used to monitor the patient's heart continuously and records asymptomatic events. New monitors are needed because they were using a very old event monitor called the King of Hearts. They don't carry parts for these anymore and the ones we had were falling apart. They were also bigger and bulkier and not easy for families to use. These monitors provide the data we need to help the hospital provide the best care possible to our patients. Each monitor will benefit about fifty patients annually.

More than 165 children from Port Alberni went to Children's Hospital last year. With this donation and the donations collected during the Port Alberni Festival of Trees, BC Children's Hospital is able to purchase 3 new ECG monitors for the hospital. The hospital continues to have other equipment needs, as well as funding needs to help build the new hospital. Please feel free to contact Steve or Barb Kalugin, at 250-723-1148 or Debbie Preston Philanthropic Coordinator at BC Children's hospital at p: 250-382-1529 c: 250-896-9621 if you are interested in making a donation.

Kris Patterson presents a cheque for $1800 to Jessica Bell, Philanthropy officer of the BC Children's Hospital Foundation Vancouver Island. Also in photo is Debbie Preston the philanthropic co-ordinator and Steve Kalugin.

Children's Hospital became a very powerful fundraising avenue for me due to the experiences I had with the loss of my daughter.

Always Cultivate an Attitude of Gratitude

GOAL SETTING

"Good thoughts are no better than good dreams unless they are executed"
– Ralph Waldo Emerson

The eagle has a small brain because the eyes are the most important. Everything else is worked around the vision. An eagle doesn't plan, it simply reacts to stimuli. We have the advantage of goal setting.

Only 3% of the population have written goals and those 3% accomplish more than the other 97% combined.

List at least 100 things you want in life. I know it is hard but by taking action on this it'll be one of the biggest determinants of success in your life. Then take that list and pick out four of the most important goals from each category of the one year, three-year, five-year and ten year goals and describe each goal in a very detailed paragraph describing why it's important to you. Be as specific as possible.

Write out your top 10 goals every day have them on index cards which you review every day. Remember to have goals that are personal, family, financial, education, spiritual, business, and social.

It is important to always have a goal in mind. Accept the fact that setbacks and obstacles will occur. But if you can visualize your goals and work towards them, one day you will achieve them. Picture your ideal life as specifically as possible and then picture yourself three years in the future having had your ideal relationship and your ideal job. Don't forget to develop goals for your future life as well. Don't spend all your time making a living instead design the life you want to live.

You should have goals in many areas including:

1) Economic goals
2) Material items you want
3) Family goals
4) Personal development goals
5) Service goals including volunteering
6) Social goals
7) Health
8) Relationships
9) Charity goals

ACTION: *The Catalyst to Achieve All Your Dreams and More*

Seven steps to goal setting

1) Decide exactly what you want and write it down.
2) Set a deadline for the goal.
3) Determine the obstacles will have to overcome to achieve the goal.
4) Determine additional skills, knowledge, abilities you will need.
5) Determine people, group and organizations will need to achieve goal.
6) Make a plan to achieve the goal.
7) Take action immediately on your plan.

We are much happier when we are fully engaged, working towards our goals. I spent most of my life drifting, never really focusing on what I wanted, instead I was reacting to whatever life presented to me. I can say that I am immensely more happy and productive when working towards a goal I want to achieve. Looking back on the things I have been able to accomplish it was by having a plan and being organized.

If you don't know where you're going any road will take you there.

101 QUESTIONS

"When you know who you are, you know what to do, you know when and where to do it and with whom." – Ralph Waldo Emerson

Self-knowledge is the basic building block of self-acceptance and self-esteem. The more you understand yourself and who you are and why you think the way you do, the more capable you are making better decisions in every area of your life. The following questions will elicit self- knowledge and put you on the path to understanding.

1) What are your skills?
2) Think of two times you failed?
3) Think of two times when you were rejected and what you learned from them?
4) What skills have you learned through new jobs or through study?
5) What activities in your work and life do you enjoy doing best?
6) If money was not a question what would you do?
7) What are you doing that is hampering your success?
8) If you could completely change places with anyone in the world would you do it? Who?
9) If you could work at anything you choose would that work be different from the work that you're doing now?
10) What are the three most important values in your life right now?
11) What are the three most important things in your life?
12) What are your three greatest accomplishments?
13) What are your three best qualities?
14) What three skills are you best at?
15) Three activities account for 90% of your success at work what are yours?
16) What have been your three biggest successes in your career?
17) Talents, abilities, temperaments are important to be used in conjunction. What are the three best jobs or parts of jobs that have used your talents, abilities, and temperament well?
18) What three job activities give you the most satisfaction?
19) If you were forced to take a significant amount of time off work and had the money how would you spend the time off? Where would you go? What would you do?

20) What are the three worst experiences you've had in your business and personal life?

21) What are the three biggest mistakes you made in your life?

22) What are the three most important lessons you learned in your life?

23) How would you change your life if you won $1 million cash tax-free tomorrow? What would you do?

24) What are your three biggest concerns or worries you have right now?

25) Who are the three people living or dead you most admire?

26) What qualities in others do you least admire?

27) What qualities in others do most admire?

28) What three words would you like people to use about you to describe you to other people?

29) If you could live anywhere in the world would you move from where you are living now?

30) If you could go back to age 12 and live your life over from that point would you do it?

31) What kind of person will I have to become to get all I want? What skills will I need? What traits will I need?

32) If you won $10 million in the lottery but only had 15 minutes to spend it or lose it what would you spend it on? The answer will tell you a lot about yourself.

33) What are the three main goals that I want to achieve this year?

34) What are three monthly goals that will move me towards my yearly intentions?

35) What are three weekly actions?

36) What are three daily outcomes?

37) How can I increase my service today?

38) What turns you off?

39) How do you relate to others?

40) Are you grateful, truly grateful?

41) What are three accomplishments you are most proud of so far?

42) What is your general view of life and the world? Are you positive and optimistic about human nature and the availabilities of opportunities or do you have a more cynical outlook?

43) What thoughts, ideas, and possibilities really motivate and excite you?

44) What are the top two distractions or energy sappers that keep you from remaining focused?

45) What causes you to get stuck in a situation or relationship?

46) What are three goals you want to accomplish in the next three months?

47) What experiences and influences do you feel have contributed most significantly to the person you are right now?

48) If you were to make a list everything you liked about any job you have done or thought about, what would be on it?

49) Who are five people whose job you would like to have and write a short paragraph describing why you want their job.

50) What are 25 things you like doing in general?

51) What are 25 things you can do or problems you can solve?

52) What are the five most important values in your life?

53) When you are free to choose how do you spend your time?

54) What are the things about your work that you like to do?

55) What brings you the greatest satisfaction?

56) What turns you on?

57) How much and what have you learned in life and have you increased your capacity for love?

58) What have been the happiest moments of your life?

59) What do you most enjoy doing in your spare time?

60) What advice would you give your child or close friends if they want to be successful in your field?

61) What is your best talent or skill?

62) What one quality would you like to develop in yourself?

63) What is the most important business lesson you have ever learned?

64) What is the most important personal lesson you have ever learned?

65) How would you change your life you found out you only had six months to live? What would be important to you? Who would you spend the time with?

66) What have you always wanted to do but were always afraid to try?

67) What activities give you a great sense of satisfaction?

68) What one great thing would you dare to dream if you knew you could not fail?

69) What do you regularly think of just before you fall asleep?

70) What one specific area of your life should you take some time to completely reevaluate your situation based on the reality of today?

71) How could you reorganize your life or work so that is more in harmony with what you want and what makes you happy?

72) How could you restructure your life or work so that you could spend more time doing the things that bring you the greatest rewards?

73) How could you simplify your life by delegating, downsizing, consolidating or eliminating low value or no value tasks or activities?

74) If you could wave a magic wand and reinvent your life completely what changes would you make?

75) In what areas of your life do you need to accept complete responsibility so that you can start moving forward?

76) What will satisfy me?

77) Do I ever recognize defeat?

78) What drives me?

79) How can I turn the negatives of my life into positives?

80) What is my ultimate goal?

81) How do you define success?

82) Are my thoughts hurting or healing?

83) Where would you like to be in 10 years?

84) What am I responsible for?

85) How can I make the world a better place?

86) Who am I?

87) Where do I want to go?

88) How do I want to be remembered?

89) Am I pursuing my dreams right now?

90) Am I sharing my skills and experiences with others?

91) What is it that people love about me?

92) Do I have a clear definition of success in my mind?

93) How do people perceive you?

94) What is the one thing that makes you special and unique?

95) If you died tomorrow, will you be happy with the life you've lived?

96) Are you a better person today than you were last year at this same time? Or 10 years ago?

97) Who is making most of the decisions of your life you, those around you or your circumstances?

98) What is the one thing you fear the most when you think of yourself as an old person?

99) What is the one movie you don't mind watching over and over again and the book that you could read over and over again?

100) What was your last random act of kindness?

101) What one action are you going to take immediately as a result of what you have learned?

What lies behind us and what lies before us are tiny matters compared to what lies within us.

Ask yourself the easy questions and you will have a hard life. Ask yourself the hard questions and you will have an easier life.

ACTION: *The Catalyst to Achieve All Your Dreams and More*

COMMUNICATION

"Communication leads to community, that is, to understanding, intimacy and mutual valuing." – Rollo May

Our attitude comes across to people through our body language and tone of voice and words. What we say is not as important as how we say it.

In face to face communication the following breakdown with percentages show the importance of non-verbal communication:

Body language 55%
Tone of voice 38%
Words 7%

It's very clear from this breakdown that non-verbal characteristics account for 93% of communication. It does change slightly on the phone because of course they don't have access to non-verbal characteristics. The percentage of what the listener actually receives is 20% words and tone of voice accounts for 80% while on the phone.

Questions can be a powerful tool to encourage dialogue. Remember to ask open ended questions. Open ended questions are questions that cannot be answered with a simple yes or no. Questions are only one half of the communication equation. You must also <u>LISTEN</u> to the answer.

Communication is a critical skill to your success. I would encourage you to undertake any endeavor which will increase your communication skills the Toastmasters program can help you hone your speaking and listening skills in a fun interactive way.

Your ability to communicate will be a key skill to your level of success in life.

The Chinese characters which make up the verb "to listen."

ACTION: *The Catalyst to Achieve All Your Dreams and More*

RELATIONSHIPS

"There's nothing greater in life then loving another and being loved in return, for loving is the ultimate of experiences." – Leo Buscaglia

The right relationship is important in your life. The right partner will share your burdens and you will achieve more than you could alone. Conversely the wrong partner will add a burden. Really take the time to think about the relationship you want to have. What does the person look like? What kind of personality do they have? The more you can describe this person, the more you will attract into your life your perfect partner.

Love is important in life and should be nurtured whenever possible, in my life I've had the privilege of finding love.

The four building blocks of love are tolerance, patience, empathy and compassion.

Needs in a relationship:

A woman's top need in a relationship is to feel safe and secure. Men primarily need to feel adequate think they are doing a good job as a boyfriend or husband

Second women need to feel like they are the center of a man's life and his attention the time. A woman needs to feel valued, to be listened to and to be showered and affection.

Finally a woman has a need for her mate totally agree with her goals so they can face the future together. Men on the other hand thrive on feeling in charge. They desire their women to give them plenty of admiration and respect

A man wants a mate who will give them a listening ear and steady companionship, someone understanding enough to appreciate him for who he is while being naughty enough to leave him feeling sexually satisfied.

List the 10 most important people in your life and write a few sentences about each one of them. What runs through your mind? What emotions do they evoke in you?

Respect is a huge component in a healthy relationship. People say the opposite of love is hate. I disagree I think it is indifference. Once indifference is allowed to seep into a relationship it very quickly leads to resentment. I encourage everyone in a relationship to discuss your feelings and to always remember how much you love and respect your partner and to remember that no argument is ever more important than loving the person you are in love with.

One of the lessons I learned from the loss of my relationship is never to take people for granted and when you find someone that you love make sure you tell them that.

Grief, Loss and Hope

"Grief is a healthy sign of our humanity and our ability to love. Through grieving we become whole again. This is not wasted time for in grief we find a way to look forward to the future again." – Leo Buscalia.

As I mentioned in my introduction I have experienced my fair share of grief and loss. In 2004 I lost my firstborn child. My daughter Ella was the most precious thing in my life. Losing her was worse than losing my own life. I spent many years struggling against the powerlessness and helplessness that I felt with that loss. It was a pain I held onto for many years. I was very fortunate to have had the support of many great people in my life including my friends, my parents and my coworkers. I would never have been able to survive the intervening years without that love and friendship. This was a very dark period of my life. I was working for minimum wage, suffering yet trying to put forth a strong image and that drained my energy. Three months after Ella passed away my appendix ruptured at work. Although I knew something was wrong I chose not to go to the hospital until approximately 14 hours later. This was not the smartest thing I have ever done, however I was at a point in my life where I no longer cared.

Several weeks after my surgery I had a health scare which required several tests. I spent approximately the next 2 months thinking that I may have had colon cancer. I found out after all the tests that everything was fine.

During this time my life was basically one crisis to another but there was one point of light in that darkness. I began a relationship with one of my coworkers named Tanya Rasanen. We had always been friends before that and she was always there and was supportive during those darkest points in my life. In April 2010 my mom was diagnosed with terminal pancreatic cancer she was told that she would have approximately 6 months to live and needless to say this devastated our family. I moved back home to help take care of my mom. During this entire time Tanya was very supportive and helped me with the arrangements and other duties. My mom succumbed to cancer on September 14, 2010. I was very worried about my father and how he would be able to cope with the loss of my mother. They were inseparable for 41 years and this loss destroyed my dad.

On May 1, 2011 I checked on my father at his house and found him with no pulse or heartbeat and he was not breathing. I immediately began CPR and did the best I could to revive him. I was unsuccessful. This began a very, very difficult part of my life. I completely felt like I had lost all meaning and was not sure which way to proceed. I had many executor duties as well as cleaning out his house, his office and dealing with a tremendous amount of paperwork. I kept myself very busy during this time as a way of not dealing with my emotions.

Throughout this time Tanya was faithfully by my side. I know for certain that I would not have been able to get through this time without her. I was unable to tell her about my feelings and how overwhelmed I was. This led to friction in our relationship and eventually caused its demise.

Tanya and I

I tell the story to reiterate how important it is to take action. Through my inaction I lost a great friend and companion. This became the turning point and the catalyst for me to change my life. I was looking for ways to transform all the negative experiences I have had and perhaps do something good with it.

I felt like I was being crushed by the losses I had felt. What I was being crushed by was the lack of dealing with things. It wasn't until I took action that things started to change. Taking on my dad's book project was a huge undertaking which required hundreds of hours of researching, editing and looking through my dad's notes. This time served two purposes. The first is that it gave me something positive to focus on rather than thinking about everything.

The second benefit is it allowed me to produce a product that people in my community have continued to enjoy and will do so for years to come.

It wasn't until after publishing my first book that I decided to take on the project of writing a book about Ella.

This book was done as a way to honor Ella and her memory as well as create some awareness for the compassionate friends organization. This is an incredible organization which is run by volunteers all of whom have lost a child. Although they are not counselors, they do offer someone to talk to. This is often a difficult thing to do especially to someone who might not have experienced that kind of loss. The book was my perspective of things that happen and I wanted to give the message that it was okay to grieve. I wanted to give an example that was okay to ask for help.

Producing the book helped my own healing, in addition to helping others. Once I took action on the book and decided to produce it, it felt like I had lost some of the pain. Earlier I did not want to give up the pain because I felt that if I let go of the pain I let go of her and that was something I could not do.

Jim Robson and I

ACTION: *The Catalyst to Achieve All Your Dreams and More*

During this time I was obsessed with self-development and personal growth which led me to read thousands of books on the subject, basically anything I get my hands on. This research uncovered some true gems of knowledge that dramatically changed and improve my life. I had already changed my mindset to become more action oriented and willingly devoured any tip or technique which would get me closer to my goal.

I finally took them time to grieve and it really helped with everything in my life. By finally giving myself permission to feel all of the hurt and pain I had been bottling up I was able to cast off a lot of the negativity making room in my life for more positive experiences.

FORGIVENESS

"The weak can never forgive. Forgiveness is the attribute of the strong." –
Mahatma Gandhi

I had many issues where forgiveness played a healing role. When my daughter
passed away there was a lot of blaming. I was the focus of this blame. I had to
let go of my anger for my own sake. I realized that holding onto my hate and
anger was only destroying me. I made a list of everybody I was angry at and
why and I then burned the list. It was a symbolic and cathartic experience. It is
amazing how much my life was changed and the rapid progress I made once I
realized the importance of letting go of past hurts.

Make a list of people you might be harbouring anger or resentment against and
one by one forgive them.

If you've had a tough childhood forgive your parents for any mistakes they may
have made in bringing you up. Everybody makes mistakes and everyone has
mistakes to forgive. This is a big step in taking personal responsibility for how
your life is going to turn out.

Learn to get past your traumas and regrets and learn how to let go. Forgive and
be free by Michael Wickett. This is an excellent program that I went through
that encouraged me to learn the power of forgiveness, gratitude and allowed me
to let go of resentments I'd been carrying for the better part of a decade.

Forgiveness will set you free to have a life of success. All your dreams can come
true.

ACTION: *The Catalyst to Achieve All Your Dreams and More*

FINANCIAL

"Money is like love; it kills slowly and painfully the one who withholds it, and enlivens the other who turns it on his fellow man." – Khalil Gibran

I was in credit card debt mainly because I had not changed my mindset in regards to money. I bought things I didn't need merely because I wasn't being the person I was meant to be. Part of my personal transformation was going from being a person owing money to a person who is debt-free and beginning to invest in real estate. The change didn't come until I changed. It was not so much a financial change as it was a personal change. When I changed what I wanted in life and what I wanted to be, the results were profound.

I went from being under employed and in debt to investing in rental real estate and other investments quite quickly once I figured out the secret of taking action and figuring out what was important in my life.

I now always try to have multiple streams of income, at least five. There should be some that are active and some that are passive so when it's slow it'll give you a chance to work on other projects.

Save 10% or more of all you earn throughout your life and invest that money accordingly. It is exclusively for savings. Always pay that 10% to yourself first before paying any other bills.

Talk to a good financial advisor; simplify your financial life, and your own home

Parkinson law states that your expenses will always rise to meet your income.

Take full advantage of compound interest and dollar cost averaging.

Investing: wealth = earnings + savings + investments

Learn to live on 70% of your net income, breaking down the remainder as follows:
10% for charity
10% for capital you need buying and fixing and selling in engaging in commerce
10% capital you provide to a financial institution for savings.

Make sure you have a wealth protection account first with a year or two of living expenses before you start to grow your money.

ACTION: *The Catalyst to Achieve All Your Dreams and More*

Decide to become financially independent.

When considering a rental property, take price of property and the rental income you will get from each month. If monthly income is above 1% look into it.

Take a sheet of paper and tally up the value of everything you have and everything you owe. Highlight your net worth. Make a promise to yourself to increase your net worth every month. Recalculate your net worth every month.

Decide to be wealthy, write down the goal and look at it every day. Today I decide to be wealthy. Take responsibility for your money. Keep a portion of everything you earn. Don't accumulate for accumulations sake. Give back.

Getting wealthy can be summed up in the phrase value creation.

FEAR

"The secret of happiness is freedom. The secret of freedom is courage." –
Thucydides 460-395 BCE

Fear is something you have to learn to master. Not eliminate – but master and direct. Fear is a good thing. It can spur a man to do the impossible or convince him to flee a danger that anger or pride or other foolish and destructive emotions might compel him to fight. I've always felt that when you feel fear it means you're on the right path. If you didn't care you would not be nervous.

Learn how to take risks and learn from them. Learn about fear management. It is important to make mistakes. The person who makes the most mistakes makes the most money and learns the most. Smart people can fear making mistakes and they never grow. Failure is the fertilizer of success.

Take a sheet of paper and write across the top one am I afraid of? Name the fear

Then ask yourself:
What is the advantage to holding on to the fear?
What price do I pay for holding onto the fear?
Where does this fear comes from?
How does this fear hold me back?
How does this fear help me?
What is the benefit to eliminating this fear?

You should master fear,
never totally banish it. Fear
can be a good thing, panic
however is destructive.

ACTION: *The Catalyst to Achieve All Your Dreams and More*

WORRY

"The only real cure for worry is purposeful action toward a predetermined goal"
– Napoleon Hill

Chronic anxiety becomes worry that if unchecked becomes more destructive. This anxiety is always caused by foolish negativism's involving failure. It is important to realize and accept the truth that one need not fear anything in this short existence. All is relative and even perception of the universe is subjective. The key to controlling fear is control of the mind for it is not emotions that affect our thinking it is improper thinking that gives birth to destructive emotions.

The following is a breakdown of things that people worry about.

Things that never happened 40%
Things over and past that can never be changed by all the worry in the world 30%
Needless worries about our health 12%
Petty miscellaneous worries 10%
Real legitimate worries 8%

92 percent of an average person's worries take up valuable time causing stress was it unnecessary instead focus on your goals and higher value activities

Make sure you enjoy the present. I spent so much time working and heading towards things I stopped enjoying the process. Whatever you're looking for must be found within you first whether it is riches, peace or happiness. Emerson said "though we travel the world over to find the beautiful, we must carry it within us or we will find it not".

You become what you think about. Fill your mind with thoughts of achieving goals instead of negativity.

One tool I have learned in my crisis intervention work which has proven to be extremely useful is what's called the 4-4-4-4 breath. This technique will lower your heart rate very quickly and allow you to regain composure. You begin inhaling for four seconds, hold that breath for four seconds, exhale for four seconds, hold the breath out for four seconds. Continue to do this breathing exercise for approximately 5 minutes and you will notice that you will feel incredibly calm and in control.

ACTION: *The Catalyst to Achieve All Your Dreams and More*

Intention without action is a promise made, intention with action is a promise kept.

Comfort zone:

I used to have a comfort zone where I knew I could not fail.
The same four walls and busy work or really more like jail.
I longed so much to do the things I've never done before.
But I stayed inside my comfort zone and paced the same old floor.

I said it didn't matter that I wasn't doing much.
I said I didn't care for things like diamonds, cars and such.
I claim to be so busy with the things inside my zone.
But deep inside I longed for some victory of my own.

I couldn't let my life go by.
Just watching others win
I held my breath and stepped outside to let the change begin.
I took a step and with a strain I'd never felt before.
I kissed my comfort zone goodbye and closed and locked the door.

If you're a comfort zone afraid to venture out
Remember that all winners at one time were filled with doubt
A step or two and words of praise can make your dreams come true
So greet your future with a smile success is there for you.

REGRETS

"Don't die with your music still inside you" – Freddie Mercury

Take more risks, don't live to be 100 wishing you did this or that add.

We were meant to express our unique gifts and regret is a great thief. I have personally lost out on many opportunities for happiness from fear and regret. This was a hallmark of my early life until I decided to do something about it.

Learn how to take risks and learn from them. Learn about fear management. It's important to make mistakes. Smart people can fear making mistakes and they never grow.

When I was going through my dad's paperwork I found an email from my mom that she had sent to him while he was at work. Even though she was in a lot of pain she talks about how 40 years have went by and she does not regret one single day. She says "I love the life I have shared with you and although it will end shorter than I expected, I want you to know I love you from the bottom of my heart. Thanks for the life we have had, I love you."

My mom devoted her life to the people she cared about, accomplished what she wanted to in life and left with no regrets. This message resonates strongly with me because I've had so very many regrets. I can't count the number of chances for happiness, joy and satisfaction I missed out on due to fear. It has certainly cost me relationships which meant quite a bit to me. I would strongly encourage you to grab life and live it to its fullest. Do not become a prisoner of your regret.

If you don't take chances you'll never get anywhere.

My mom & dad who were inseparable for 40 years

ACTION: *The Catalyst to Achieve All Your Dreams and More*

The Dilemma

To laugh is to risk appearing the fool,
To weep is to risk appearing sentimental,
To reach out for another is to risk involvement,
To expose feelings is to risk rejection.

To place your dreams before the crowd is to risk ridicule,
To love is to risk not being loved in return,
To go forward in the face of overwhelming odds is to risk failure,
But risks must be taken because the greatest hazard in life is to risk nothing.

The person who risks nothing, does nothing, has nothing, is nothing
He may avoid suffering but he cannot learn, feel, change, grow or love.
Chained by his certitudes he is a slave he has forfeited his freedom.
Only a person who takes risks is free.

PERSISTENCE

"When the night is darkest, the stars come out" – Ralph Waldo Emerson

A journey of 1000 miles begins with a single step. Many can walk the mile but few can travel that final inch.

In 2009 I decided to take action and complete the Great Lake Ultra Marathon. I wanted to prove to myself that I could do it after the car accident. I wanted to prove I was not a cripple and did not have to give in and live my life according to the limitations imposed on me by the actions of a careless person. I also had the intention of combining it into a fundraiser for my daughter and children's hospital. I knew that if I did it only for me I could fail, but by linking up to something bigger than myself I had that extra motivation. It was a difficult challenge I set for myself. I had done little to no preparation for this ultra-marathon but I was utterly convinced I was going to be able to complete the event. It is a 56 km walk from Youbou to Lake Cowichan which takes place annually in September. I set the goal of finishing no matter what, even if I had to crawl across the finish line. I wanted to quit many times but I would say to myself "one more step" and "one more step" and I made it. I remember at approximately kilometer 35 I felt like I had nothing left inside me and all I wanted to do was quit. I was forced to look inside myself and reach inside for the motivation to continue. The ability to reach inside yourself and persevere teaches you can always go beyond your own limits. You can derive quite a bit of power from learning this. I blew up a photo of me reaching the finish line and ringing the bell and had it framed. It hangs on my wall to remind me of when things get tough and everything seems hard that I can do it and that photo has become an anchor for that state of mind. I can look at that photo and remember the feelings of success and accomplishment.

This is the photo of me ringing the bell at the finish line.

ACTION: *The Catalyst to Achieve All Your Dreams and More*

Often when you think you can't do anymore and you feel discouraged and want to quit this is often the time when you break through to great achievements.

Don't quit

When things go wrong, as they sometimes will
When the road you're trudging seems all up hill.
When funds are low and the debts are high,
And you want to smile, but you had to sigh.

When care is pressing you down a bit,
Rest, if you must, but don't you quit.
Life is queer with its twists and turns,
As every one of us sometimes learns.

And many a failure turns about
When he might have won had he stuck it out:
Don't give up though the pace seems slow.
You may succeed with another blow.

Success is failure turned inside out
The silver tint of the clouds of doubt.
And you never can tell how close you are.
It may be near when it seems so far:

So stick to the fight when you're hardest hit.
It's when things seem worst that you must not QUIT.

Author unknown.

LIFELONG LEARNING

"Anyone who stops learning is old, whether at 20 or 80. Anyone who keeps learning stays young." – Henry Ford

I completed a diploma in adult psychology and child psychology as well as courses in fitness and nutrition, lock-smithing and several other courses. I have incorporated useful elements from these courses into my life as well.

You must keep up your education throughout your life. I spent a bit of time learning how to learn. As part of that I learnt about learning styles and how I learn best. Take the time to figure out which learning modality is best suited to you. Whether your style is visual, audio, or kinesthetic, learning this about yourself will dramatically increase your learning capacity and therefore also your quality of life. Also learn how other people take in information because it is important to connect with people the way they best connect.

I have really been passionate about learning and applying more and more of what I have learned. I have learned a lot but once I started taking action I became amazed at what I have accomplished. I constantly expose myself to new ideas and strategies and apply them. If they don't work out then they are discarded. I have also looked for ideas that will help increase my other skills exponentially. I do regret that I never looked inside myself before this and how much more I could have accomplished.

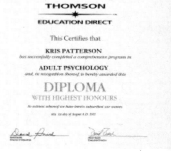

DISCIPLINE

"Discipline is the bridge between goals and accomplishment" – Jim Rohn

Discipline is an important trait for success. It was something I was sorely lacking in my life. My success in life came in in direct proportion the forming of certain daily habits. The first of which is my power hour. This is where I spend at least 60 minutes listening to inspirational audio programs or writing in my journal or thinking about my goals etc. After that I immediately spend 60 to 90 minutes in uninterrupted writing I have held down a job during this period where I was working at least 60 hours per week. I found that when something is important to you and you realize how valuable it is, you make the time for it.

Many people complain about having no time and then they watch TV for hours every day. One of the most productive things you can do is to get rid of your TV. They say at the end of your life a person who is 75 years old has wasted approximately 8 years of their life watching TV. Imagine all the things you can do with those eight years. You could earn a doctorate in a subject that appeals to you. I decided to cut off my television cable. I hadn't realized how much time I was wasting on television. I originally cut it off because I was paying too much for something I wasn't really using. After cutting off my cable I found I did have extra time which allowed me to complete two books simultaneously.

I also began the habit of listening to instructional audio programs in my car using my commute and driving time more constructively.

Discipline is something that changed my life. I looked at the things in my life that were missing and I looked for ways to incorporate them into my life.

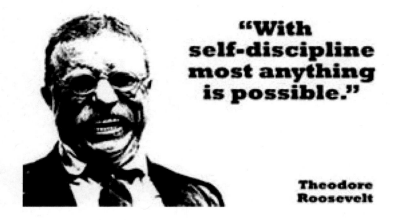

"With self-discipline most anything is possible."

Theodore Roosevelt

ACTION: *The Catalyst to Achieve All Your Dreams and More*

TIME MANAGEMENT

"He, who plans the transactions of the day, and follows out that plan, carries a thread that will guide him through the labyrinth of the most busy life. But where no plan is laid, where the disposal of time is surrendered merely to the chance of incidents, all things lie huddled together in one chaos." – Victor Hugo

People all have the same amount of time. I have heard many people say they don't have enough time. We have the same amount of time as say, Einstein, Newton, and Leonardo Da Vinci and look what they were able to do with their twenty-four hours.

How do you start your day?

I start my day with the first two hours working on projects that are directly beneficial to my primary goal and objective. During this time I also listen to self-improvement audio programs and try to read something uplifting and inspirational. I spent years hitting the alarm clock, getting up and just rushing out to get to work. I found through personal experience I am a much more productive person when I start my day in a more beneficial manner. This way no matter what happens I know I have achieved something before most people have even woken up. I personally commit to 6-8 AM in the morning. I generally put in another hour after work as well. I work through lunch and work extra hours as well. Part of this discipline comes from the fact that I enjoy what I do for a living. I admit this is a rather extreme schedule for someone to commit to, however I have had a driving passion to grow and had a terrific amount of learning to do and material to work through. I noticed a change in my life by following this schedule. Within a year I published two books while working at least sixty hours a week, fulfilled the duties of an executor and listened to several hundred hours of audio instruction. I was also able to read many books, and synthesize this knowledge into something that was actionable. I also began actively sharing my knowledge with my sales team. I've always believed that if you want to learn something twice teach it once.

One hour a day on weekdays: Ensure that you are reading for one hour a day. That works out to approximately one book a week on average or 50 books a year. Remember the average North American reads less than three books per year. Commit to lifelong learning, take every seminar you can, read everything you get your hands on which will help you become a better person. Take a blank sheet of paper and at the top of the page write your present primary goal clearly and simply. Next write down as many ideas as you can for improving the job in which you are employed. An hour a day, five days a week totals 260 hours a year

ACTION: *The Catalyst to Achieve All Your Dreams and More*

This increases your service six full extra working weeks a year, time devoted to thinking and planning, this alone will put you far above your competition.

Time can't be saved only spent
Time is in dispensable all work requires time
Time is irreplaceable
Time is essential
You can't manage time you can only manage yourself.
Priorities and posteriorities
A, B, C, D, E method delegate and eliminates

Top 10 time eaters
Crisis management
Telephone interruptions
Lack of objectives and priorities planning
Attempting too much
Ineffective delegation
Drop-in visitors
Personal disorganization
Lack of self-discipline
Procrastination
Inability to say no

Decide what you want and write it down

"There are some who say that time itself is a hammer: that each slow second marks another tap that makes big rocks into little rocks, waterfalls into canyons, cliffs into beaches.

There are some who say that time is instead a blade. They see the dance of its razored tip, poised like a venomous snake, forever ready to slay faster than the eye can see.

And there are some who say that time is both hammer and blade. They say the hammer is a sculptor's mallet, and the blade is a sculptor's chisel: that each stroke is a refinement, a perfecting, a discovery of truth and beauty within what would otherwise be a blank and lifeless stone".– Matthew Stover.

Time management if you can control your time you can control your life.

PRODUCTIVITY

"When you waste a moment, you have killed it in a sense, squandering an irreplaceable opportunity. But when you use the moment properly, filling it with purpose and productivity, it lives on forever." – Menachem Mendel Schneerson

Write down the six most important things you have to do today number them and prioritize them and don't start item to until number one is finished.

30, 60, 90 strategy: This is a very simple idea where you pick a project and give it your total focus for 30, 60, or 90 minutes. This is not a time for you to multitask. Turn your phone off, don't check your emails, do nothing but work solely on that project. I begin my day with a 90 minute block of time dedicated to my primary goal. This is something that takes some self-discipline but eventually it will become a habit.

Take a vacation every year it helps to have a clear perspective and will actually make you a more productive employee. It helps with perspective this lesson took me many years to learn. I was running a martyr mindset for many years thinking killing myself or my company was the way to get ahead. I felt better and have more creative ideas when I spent time away from the office. You never know when inspiration will strike you sometimes one needs to get away and look at things from the outside. Schedule your vacations ahead of time and stick to them.

Ask yourself who are the top three or four people in your company ask them out to lunch or dinner and ask them to teach you some of the things that you can do differently

Every day try to productively do something in the following areas:
1) Work
2) Physical i.e. exercise, running, swimming
3) Social
4) Creativity or education: whether it's writing, making music, cooking, taking classes, etc.
5) Relaxation: whether it's reading a book or watching a TV whatever it is that you find to be relaxing.

There are 6000 waking hours in a year. 2000 hours are spent on the job. That leaves you with 4000 hours where you are neither sleeping nor working. What are you doing with your time?

ACTION: *The Catalyst to Achieve All Your Dreams and More*

Breakdown dreams into goals, goals into steps, steps into tasks.

Letting go of the past: A lot of people spend time dwelling on the past and allowing negative experiences to continue to influence their lives in a bad way.

Daily habits:
Prioritize day
Gratitude and achievement which reminds you of how rich your life is
Think of five things that are truly grateful for
What did you accomplish today?
What have I planned for tomorrow?

Five questions for success:
What am I most excited about?
What makes me happy?
What can I do today to get me closer to my goals?
Who loves me in my life?
What can I do today to make other people happy?

Take one hour a day with a completely blank piece of paper and write down one of your primary goals clearly and concisely than think about as many different ways to improve at what you do for a living.

After action review:
What were your three greatest accomplishments this year?
Analyze what you learned from each accomplishment
What were your biggest disappointments from the last year?
What did you learn from this failure?
Analyze how you limited yourself and how you can stop it
Were there certain actions you took or didn't take that came back to haunt you?

Pragmatically review all of the information you have gathered. This will help you know yourself better and how you can improve.

Use this information to astonish yourself in the next year.

Year review highlights lessons learned, how I evolved, memorable moments and various goals I've advanced toward.

The year past

1) What went well?
2) In what ways did I grow and evolve: how were you tested or challenged and how did I grow as a result?
3) What were my favourite moments of ?
4) What do I need to clean out or let go of now to be ready to start fresh in?
5) What and who am I most grateful for right now?
6) If there was a theme for the last year what was it?
7) What are my goals for the year?
8) Which of my strengths and assets will I tap into to realize my goals?
9) How will I foster my personal well-being to maintain or boost my mojo?
10) What new skills will I acquire or deepen?
11) How can I contribute to the greater good?
12) What will my theme be for the coming year?

Leverage: learn how to utilize other people's experiences and time. It is always better to learn from mistakes. If you can learn from someone else's why reinven the wheel.

Health

The 8, 8, 20 rule: eight hours of sleep, eight glasses of water and at least 20 minutes of direct face to sky contact with the sun each day.

Keep your mind sharp at all times. Read biographies of people you are interested in or have done what you want to achieve.

Remember the importance of sleep. There are a lot of adverse health risks to no getting enough of the right amount of sleep and rest.

Walk for 1000 steps each night after dinner. The Chinese believe if you walked thousand steps each night after dinner you can live to be 150.

ACTION: *The Catalyst to Achieve All Your Dreams and More*

HOARDER

*"Anything you can't relinquish when it has outlived its usefulness possesses
you and in this materialistic age many of us are possessed by our possessions."*
– Mildred Norman

I had a tendency to hold on to things so much so that I was worried I would
become a hoarder. Along with the other things I've done to change my life
around was to think about why I had these tendencies and by understanding
these I was able to transform things from the root rather than just getting rid
of things and starting all over again with a new series of attachments. I took the
time to analyze my life in its entirety. I knew it was time to redesign my life how
I wanted to be rather just reacting to what came into my life. The best way to do
this is getting rid of everything and putting back only what fits into your design.

If one changes internally, one should not continue to live with the same objects.
They reflect one's mind and psyche of yesterday. I throw away what has no
dynamic living use.

Clutter creates stress. Just looking at clutter suggests clutter to the mind. Spend
5 to 10 minutes every day devoted to the de-cluttering of something.

I had many possessions which I'd had for years and never used for example
books and audio programs. It feels like these possessions just sitting around
have gotten power over me. With each item I use or let go of, I reclaim a little
of my personal power. In one year I gave away a lot of my books and audio
programs to charity and to people who could use them. I was holding onto
these items because I connected them to important times in my life and formed
a strong emotional attachment to the item. Once I made this realization I
understood I could let these items go and it doesn't take anything away from
who I am. More people will enjoy these books and the knowledge will be used
and given to someone. Who knows who they will give them to, where they will
end up and who they will influence?

I spent a lot of years buying things because I thought I wanted them. I realize
now I didn't buy those things because I wanted them but was instead trying to
fill some void in my life. I know that the answer is to understand you are already
perfect without needing these extraneous things. They are just objects. The
secret to life is simplifying. I spent a year eliminating a lot of my possessions,
returning to the essentials. I was terrified to give up these possessions years
ago, but I made the discovery that these items were holding back my growth
and that made the transition easier. Some people suggest you sell all of your
extra stuff. That is one option I donated the vast majority of my books to a

local literacy organization. They have a program which they call little libraries. These are receptacles placed around our town where people can take a book or leave a book. These are stations that will be used to increase literacy and encourage reading. I made a donation of several hundred books to help them get this program started. It has become a cornerstone of one of my philosophies to help someone with everything I do. I had bought so many books which had remained unread and I set a goal to read them and donate the ones I wasn't keeping to this program. I know that these books will encourage others. I'd already harvested the knowledge from these books and was holding onto them for no real reason and now they have a new life inspiring others.

I had a tendency toward procrastination. I've been holding onto every item on the off chance I was still going to use it. I do recommend that you be ruthless with what you choose to keep and give away. The more you simplify the more time you have to focus on the really important stuff in your life. That's why it's so important to have your goals and dreams clearly defined.

Action Success Habits And Thoughts

"The chains of habit are too light to be felt until they are too heavy to break."
– Warren Buffett

- Make a list as big as you can about everything you appreciate about yourself and achievements you are proud of then share the list with someone else. This will go a long way to improving your self-esteem and confidence in life

- Don't become hung up whether you think you're good bad or indifferent. Don't concern yourself with whether you're better or worse than other people.

- Information alone is not transformation

- Learn how to be present. Mindfulness will add to everything you do. I always left things unfinished so I was surrounded by unfinished projects and this defeated me. I was always thinking of other things rather than concentrating on the project that I was working on. I felt way better once I started completing projects and reclaiming my time

- Indecision is the greatest thief of opportunity (Jim Rohn)

- Every mistake I made in life is one where I thought twice.

- 83% of all decisions should be made right away.

- Of all the factors that successful people had, speed of implementation was the most important.

- The best day is always the one you're in.

- Every problem you face is a gift which is a valuable lesson. Like a guardian angel that sends you exactly what you need to learn, exactly when you need to learn it.

- It is incredible reclaiming your power once you have conquered your past and allowed it to hold you up rather than weighing you down.

- Journaling has also helped me through many crises is in my life. It gives you a chance to reflect on your life years later and shows the progress you've made and the lessons you have learned.

- Year in review DVD program: This is something I started approximately 10 years ago. The process is very simple. I reflect on all of my accomplishments and achievements throughout the year. I gather photos which represent those achievements. Once I have all of the photos that I'm going to use in the DVD which is usually around 60 I create a DVD slideshow put to music. I used to only include positive achievements but now I also included things that were difficult, challenges that happened during the year that I was able to persevere through. This process allows you to think about what you did during the year, what lessons you learned, what you'd like to work on in the next year and it really encapsulates your year and the lessons learned. I then watch this two minute DVD a few times back to back absorbing the wisdom of that year.

- Increase your education. Grow your own personal library. Buy your own books and mark them up that way if you want to review the important parts it won't take long. Take the important parts than type up your notes for review later.

- Read in your field for 30 to 60 minutes each day and think throughout the day of how you can use what you've learned. If you do that each day you should be completing one book per week. The average North American reads less than three books per year. If you read one book per week you should finish at least 50 books each year. Earning a PhD from a major university requires the reading and synthesis into a dissertation of about 40 to 50 books.

- The average person spends 500 to 1000 hours each year in his or her vehicle. This is the equivalent of 3 to 6 months of 40 hour weeks or the equivalent of one or two university semesters. Make sure you're using this time to your best advantage by listening to audio programs in your vehicle.

- The power hour this is the term I have used to describe the one hour I spend every morning before getting into my day. I use this hour to grow myself professionally and personally. This is time spent listening to audio programs, journaling, reading or just thinking about what my goals are and different ways to accomplish more. I found that when I spend the hour this way my days go way better and I get more done in my day-to-day life. I'm a much more focused person. I used to get up, jump into the day rush to work and I always felt rushed. This way of easing into the day has definitely made me a better person which in turn has increased my service in my community. I have encouraged everyone I know to make this our part of the day as well. Several of my friends have turned their lives around with his hour being the turning point.

- Build your personal library which reflects your passions and interests. Also make your journals part of your library. Your journals contain your reflections on life, lessons you have learned, books you have read your thoughts and feelings if it's worth living it's worth writing down.

- The path to success is to take massive determined action. Take action on your own life.

- Gems are polished by rubbing just as men and women are made brilliant by trials.

- Golf balls originally used to be smooth. Golfers found that the balls that they had hit over and over again developed dimples from where they'd been struck. It turns out the balls that have been smacked around the most flew faster and farther than the smooth ones. The lesson here is that we too can suffer bumps and bruises along the way during the course of our lives, and these experiences can make us better for having had them.

- A body in motion tends to stay in motion conversely a body at rest tends to stay at rest get up take action and experience the power of momentum.

- Unhappiness starts with doing a little less than you can.

- Service to many leads to greatness. If you can help enough people get what they want you can get everything you want.

- The great secret to success is that there are no secrets

- Formal education will make you a living; self-education will make you a fortune.

- The secret is you really can do, be and have anything you want no matter where you are today. You need only one thing to get all of them. And that one thing is self-discipline.

- Mind storming: Write a problem down and come up with 20 ideas on how to solve it. Then take out one of the ideas and take action on it immediately.

- Make an accomplishments wall in your office where you can see what you have done and things that you are proud of. Also do a dream wall with things you would like to accomplish. I have a picture of me rain the bell at the finish line of the great Lake walk, a framed letter from the mayor among many others whenever I feel down about things I think about these things and what they represent. They represent much more than mere paper they are anchors to the knowledge I have been in difficult situations and when it seemed like when it was the only option I persevered and accomplished something. You gather power occasions when you dig deep and find out what you have inside

- What you like to do between the ages of 7 to 14 are a good indicator of what you would be best suited to do as an adult.

- On the beach of hesitation lies the bleached bones of people who at the moment of victory paused.

- Experience is a hard teacher because she gives you the test first, the lesson afterward. Vernon Law.

- An ounce of action is worth a ton of theory (Frederick Engels)

- Fortune extends her hand to the daring man, kissed the dainty hand of fate and she will lead you forever more.

- The More you try the more likely you are to triumph

- Insight without action makes no difference.

- To get more you have to be more

- Your level of service determines your reward or you reap what you sow

- It's better to burn out than to fade away (Neil Young)

- Avoiding danger is no safer in the long run than outright exposure. Life is either a daring adventure or nothing. (Helen Keller)

- All of life is action and passion and not to be caught up in the actions and passions of one's time is to run the risk of not having truly lived. (Herodotus)

- Figure out your likes and dislikes, strengths and weaknesses.

- Read as much as you can, practice writing by keeping a journal, writing stories or jotting down ideas as they come to you.

- List everything you liked about any job you have done or thought about

- Think about five people whose job would like to have. Write a short paragraph describing why you want the job.

- One of the habits that I've got myself into several years ago is I listen to Earl Nightingale's program lead the field. I take a day and I listen to the program in its entirety in one sitting. I do this to remind myself of certain important things and I found this program to be quite life-changing every time I listen to it I seem to get some new insight from it.

ACTION: *The Catalyst to Achieve All Your Dreams and More*

- Build your personal library which reflects your passions and interests. Also make your journals part of your library. Your journals contain your reflections on life, lessons you have learned, books you have read your thoughts and feelings. If it's worth living its worth writing down.

- The most important ability is responsibility.

- Decide to be successful. A lot of people have the idea of being successful of having a lot of money but never decide to do it. Get clear about what success means to you and make a plan to go and get it.

- Craft a mission statement and remember you are 100% responsible for your life and career.

- The more you do, the more you will find you can do. The less you do the harder it gets to do anything.

- The best helping hand you will ever find is at the end of your own arm.

- Become action oriented.

- You are 100% responsible for your life and career.

- Set aside one hour every morning for personal development matters. Meditate, visualize your day, read inspirational texts, listen to audio programs, watch the sunrise once a week or be with nature.

- There was a fire in Yellowstone National Park and they thought it would destroy the park and the heat the fire released was actually the catalyst necessary to release the ability of the lodge pole pine tree to actually spread. Nature deals with adversity by constantly renewing itself and reinventing itself that's a lesson that we can all hope to learn.

- The price of inaction is far greater than the cost of making a mistake. (Meister Eckhart)

- There are risks in cost to a program of action but they are far outweighed by the long-term risks and costs of comfortable inaction (John F. Kennedy)

- Set aside Sunday evenings for yourself. Use this time to plan your week to visualize your encounters hope to achieve to read new materials to listen to soft soothing music and to relax. Be disciplined with this habit.

- Slip from moment to moment like a snake sheds its old skin. He does not try to carry the old skin with him. The man of awareness has no cargo, he moves unencumbered. Be like a dewdrop that slips from the blade of grass.

- Embrace kaizen which is Japanese for continuous improvement. Basically it means that you can accomplish incredible things by becoming a tiny bit better each day.

- Success is more of a subtraction process than it is an additive process. We already have all we need inside us. Success is simply a matter of removing the beliefs, attitudes, and habits that get in our way. (Bill Grove)

- Have a future orientation always have clear written goals for the next 3 to 5 years. Always have a long-term perspective.

- Be goal oriented have your goals in writing and review them daily.

- Be results oriented

- Be excellence orientation focus on becoming absolutely excellent in every area of endeavor.

- People orientation: Relationships both personal and business are critical in life.

- Action orientation: become intensely action oriented in everything you do. Have a sense of urgency a bias towards action.

- Life is filled with tests one after another and if you don't recognize that you are certain to fail the most important ones.

ACTION: *The Catalyst to Achieve All Your Dreams and More*

A PARADOX OF OUR TIME IN HISTORY

Although counterculture comedian George Carlin is often credited for writing this poignant piece after the death of his wife, the actual author is a Christian minister. According to an article in the rumor mill, the author of this piece is Dr. Bob Moorehead, former pastor of Seattle's Overlake Christian Church. It was included in a 1995 collection called words aptly spoken.

Regardless of who wrote it, this article is worth reprinting.

The paradox of our time in history is that we have taller buildings but shorter tempers, wider freeways but narrower viewpoints. We spend more, but have less, we buy more, but enjoy less. We have bigger houses and smaller families, more conveniences, but less time. We have more degrees but less sense, more knowledge but less judgment, more experts, yet more problems, more medicine, but less wellness.

We drink too much, smoke too much, spend too recklessly, laugh too little, drive too fast, get too angry, stay up too late, get up too tired, read too little, watch TV too much and pray too seldom. We have multiplied our possessions but reduced our values. We talk too much, love too seldom and hate too often.

We've learned how to make a living, but not a life. We've added years to life not life to years. We've been all the way to the moon and back, but have trouble crossing the street to meet a new neighbor. We conquered outer space but not inner space. We've done larger things but not better things.

We've cleaned up the air, but polluted the soul. We've conquered the atom, but not our prejudice. We write more, but learn less. We plan more, but accomplish less. We've learned to rush, but not to wait. We build more computers to hold more information, to produce more copies than ever, but we communicate less and less.

These are the times of fast foods and slow digestion, big men and small character, steep profits and shallow relationships. These are the days of two incomes but more divorce, fancier houses, but broken homes. These are the days of quick trips, disposable diapers, throwaway morality, one night stands, overweight bodies, and pills that do everything from cheer, to quiet, to kill. It is a time when there is much in the showroom window and nothing in the stock room. A time when technology can bring this letter to you, and a time when you can choose either to share this insight, or to just hit delete.

ACTION: *The Catalyst to Achieve All Your Dreams and More*

Remember; spend some time with your loved ones, because they are not going to be around forever.

Remember, say a kind word to someone who looks up to you in awe, because that little person soon will grow up and leave your side.

Remember, to give a warm hug to the one next to you, because that is the only treasure you can give with your heart and it doesn't cost a cent.

Remember, to say I love you to your partner and your loved ones, but most of all mean it. A kiss and an embrace will mend hurt when it comes from deep inside of you.

Remember to hold hands and cherish the moment for someday that person will not be there again.

Give time to love, give time to speak, and give time to share the precious thoughts in your mind.

And always remember:

Life is not measured by the number of breaths we take, but by the moments that take our breath away.

CONCLUSION:

I'm in no way shape or form perfect. I have made more than my fair share of mistakes and worse I've made many of the same mistakes over and over again. It wasn't until I took the time to figure this all out that my life changed for the better.

One cannot learn wisdom by sitting at another's feet. One must live one's own life, make one's own mistakes and feel one's own ecstasy to learn the true meaning of existence, for it is different in each individual. Fall down, get up and do it all over again. Experience and learn that is the only way.

I know you have great ideas that you can share with people. I hope that this book will help give you the confidence and the impetus to look inside yourself for the answers and take action. I provided several tools to teach you about yourself. I recommend that you purchase a separate notebook to record your ideas and answers to the questions and exercises in this book

This book isn't meant to be a self-help book per se because those types of books imply that you have a deficit. The objective of this book is to reveal to you, that you just have to take action to reveal how truly great you already are.

You get out of life what you put into it. Audio programs and books point the way but you need to take action. They give you tips, tools and techniques but you need to put in the effort.

I'm interested in hearing from you. Stories, comments, and questions are always welcome and can be emailed to me at kris@krispatterson.com. I would also encourage you to check out my website at krispatterson.com to see more of my book projects.

The path to success is to take massive determined action. Take action on your life and make all of your dreams come true.

Acknowledgments

I would like to thank the usual people, Phil Littlewood most of all of course. I don't think any project I've ever done would be complete without Phil's involvement and expertise. I'd also like to thank Christopher Finlayson for the back cover photo. I'd also like to thank not another person but a realization. It is both known and expected that several parts of this book may incite conflicting feelings within the reader as several of the concepts are designed to do just that. But this stirring up is precisely the threshold experience that we are trying to engender. It does remain the responsibility of the motivated reader to form and channel these feelings to productive ends, a task no book is able to accomplish in and of itself. Take action and enjoy the experience.

RESOURCES

This book is from my experience of things I've done to turn my life around. These are some of the things that I have found to be effective. I went through thousands of books and audio programs and courses, the best of these have been included here.

I learned many things from my parents. My mom was the first publisher of the daily newspaper in my community in an almost 100 year history. From her I learned a lot about the publishing industry as well as her ability to get things done. She was never one to let your realities get in the way of doing what was right.

I learned a lot about sales for my dad as well along with that he taught me how to make decisions. He taught me about always making the right decision for everybody concerned sometimes we have to choose between the light we stand in and the light we all stand. Both my parents instilled in me a sense of community and how we should always remember where we came from.

One of the other things I did in my process of self-growth was signed up for Brian Tracy's personal mentoring success program through the Nightingale Conant Corporation. This consisted of approximately 30 CDs and entire workbook to work through this began as the beginning changing point in my life. Working through this program allowed me to help design the life I wanted rather than merely allowing stuff to happen to me. Once I started taking control of my life the change began very quickly.

Music and nature have been inspirational to me and have left their mark on this work.

Four minute fitness program: This was a class I attended with Dr. Keith Jefferies. He created a program that combines tai chi breathing visualization and other characteristics to form a system that can be performed in four minutes and will really change your life. I recommend that everybody gets a chance to become familiar with the system. It became part of my daily life.

The Richest Man in Babylon: George Klassen. This book which has very simple theories which if applied will change your financial life.

Forgive and be free Michael Wickett: I worked through this audio program a few years ago and I really worked it, completing all of the exercises. It really helped me change my life allowed me to let go of a lot of stuff me back. This allowed me to create space in my life are more positive experiences and outcomes.

ACTION: *The Catalyst to Achieve All Your Dreams and More*

Conquering Procrastination: Neil Fiore

Tony Robbins personal power program the driving force: I bought this program many years ago on cassettes at a used bookstore. When I began going through my period of change and transition I listened to the program in its entirety. I particularly found the Dickens exercise was very powerful for me. I had this program for about 12 years sitting in my attic. It wasn't until after the passing of my father that I made a concerted effort and decided finish the program in its entirety. This was one of the programs I always meant to listen to but had never been able to. Completing this program was one of the originating sparks in transforming my life.

I did utilize other programs along the way as well but this original Tony Robbins program was one that started it. It helped consolidate a lot of the thoughts I've been having up to that point and give them something to focus towards.

The Four Laws of Financial Freedom

The war of art: Stephen Pressfield. The book is great in its entirety however the discussions on resistance were life changing for me.

Secrets of 10 great geniuses: Tony Alessandra

Getting things done: David Allen

Think and grow rich audio and book version

The Way of the Bull: by Leo Buscaglia

Love: by Leo Buscaglia

Loving Each Other: by Leo Buscaglia

The science of personal achievement audio series

Maximum Confidence: Jack Canfield: This is an audio program covers a lot of where self-esteem comes from.

The Artists Way: Julia Cameron

Ready fire aim by Michael Masterson

Seven habits of successful people by Stephen Covey

The Magic of Thinking Big: David Schwarz

Life was never meant to be a struggle Stuart Wilde

The relaxation response Herbert Benson

The automatic millionaire.

Millionaire messenger by Brendan Bouchard. It will show you a lot of good tips and strategies the get your book ideas and your personal message and make them a reality.

Book of five rings Miyamoto Musashi

The art of war: Sun Tzu

Man's search for meaning Viktor Frankel

Everything by:
Earl Nightingale
Jim Rohn
Brian Tracy
Dennis Waitely
Robin Sharma

SUPPLEMENTAL APPENDIX

Seven disciplines for success:
1) Goal setting
2) Time management
3) Balance family and work
4) Good health diet exercise and rest
5) Continuous learning: knowledge is the raw material of success in the information age.
6) Regular savings and investment of your income
7) Honesty and integrity

Seven rules for the 21st century
1) Your life only gets better when you get better
2) It doesn't matter where you came from only where you're going.
3) Whatever is worth doing is worth doing poorly at first.
4) You are only as free as your options.
5) Every difficulty offers a seed to a greater opportunity.
6) You can learn anything you need to learn.
7) Only limits on what you can do or be are the ones you accept.

10 steps to stop procrastinating
1) List what you are putting off
2) Do one task right away
3) Set designated time to start task
4) Beat boredom by using your mind
5) Imagine you have only one year to live
6) Don't worry about perfection
7) Say "i will_"
8) If what you are putting off involves other people, consult with them
9) If your fear the consequences for the action, ask yourself what is the very worst thing can happen
10) Vividly picture how free you will feel once the task is completed

Nine steps to problem solving:
1) Define the problem
2) Write down everything you know about the problem
3) Decide what people and resources to bring into the solution
4) Make a note of everything that is related to the problem
5) Conduct a brainstorming session by yourself
6) Conduct a brainstorming session in a group
7) Evaluate the ideas for the best options

8) Create an action plan

9) Give yourself a deadline to put the plan into action.

10 questions for establishing rapport:
1) How did you get started in?
2) What do you enjoy most about what you do?
3) What separates your company from your competition?
4) What advice would you give to someone just starting out in your business?
5) What one thing would you do with your business if you knew you could not fail?
6) What significant changes have you seen take place since you started in this industry?
7) What do you see is the coming trends in your business? This question allows the person to speculate.
8) Describe the funniest or strangest experience in your business. This gives them the chance to tell their war stories?
9) What ways have you found the most effective in promoting your business?
10) What one sentence would you like people to use in describing your business?

Seven success principles:
1) Clarity is essential
2) Responsibility is absolute
3) Learning is continuous school is never out for professionals
4) Relationships are everything
5) Creativity is unlimited
6) Time is precious
7) Success is inevitable

Affirmations for building self-esteem
1. I am a valuable person and worthy of the respect of others.
2. I am optimistic about life! I look forward to and enjoy new challenges to my awareness
3. I am my own expert and i allow others the same privilege.
4. I express my ideas easily and i know that there are others who respect my point of view
5. I am aware of my values and confident in the decisions i make based on my awareness
6. I have pride in my past performance and a positive expectancy for the future
7. I bounce back quickly from disappointments
8. I can accept compliments and i can share success
9. I am a unique and therefore precious being

ACTION: *The Catalyst to Achieve All Your Dreams and More*

10. I am actively in charge of my life and i direct it in constructive channels
11. I realize that love is letting go of fear and grievances
12. It is not what happens to me but _how_ i handle it that determines my
    emotional well-being.
13. I love myself, and like myself, i am ok
14. I am an action person, doing first things first and one thing at a time
15. I treat everyone with warmth and respect.
16. I am gentle with myself
17. I can make mistakes and still remain a valuable and worthwhile person
18. I forgive myself and others easily
19. I am responsible for the way i see and react to the world around me
20. I feel strong, competent and capable

12 things to remember
The value of time
The success of perseverance
The pleasure of working
The dignity of simplicity
The worth of character
The power of example
The influence of life
The obligation of duty
The wisdom of economy
The virtue of patience
The improvement of talent
The joy of originating

Advice for Life

- Advice
- Never give up on your dreams
- Holding grudges only prolongs the pain
- Know who you are and stay true to it
- Respect other people's philosophies but choose your own path.
- Listen to your mentors.
- Live for something don't drift through life emotionlessly
- Put passion into whatever you do.
- Always look for the positive side of things.
- Darkness is only the absence of light, you have four other senses.
- Let go of the past.
- Don't be too proud to accept help
- Trust your instincts.

- Accept don't expect
- Live on less
- Love more
- Laugh in the mirror
- Contribute your innate gifts
- Value yourself
- Seek universal truth
- Have clean motives
- Focus your commitments
- Discover balance
- Serve others

Advice for coping with anxiety that is 300 years old

Go placidly amid the noise and haste and remember what peace there may be in silence.

As far as possible without surrender be on good terms with all persons.

Speak your truth quietly and clearly and listen to others even the dull and ignorant they too have their story.

Avoid loud and aggressive persons; they are vexatious to the spirit.

If you compare yourself with others you may become vain and bitter for always there'll be greater and lesser persons than yourself.

Enjoy your achievements as well as your plans.
Keep interested in your own career however humble it is a real possession in the changing fortunes of time.

Exercise caution in your business affairs for the world is full of trickery but let this not blind you to what virtue there is, many persons strive for high ideals and everywhere life is full of heroism.

Be yourself especially do not feign affection neither be cynical about love for the face of all aridity and disenchantment it is as perennial as the grass.

Take kindly the Council of the years gracefully surrendering the things of youth.

Nurture strength of spirit to shield you in sudden misfortune but do not distress yourself with imaginings many fears are born of fatigue and loneliness.

ACTION: *The Catalyst to Achieve All Your Dreams and More*

Beyond a wholesome discipline be gentle with yourself you are a child of the universe no less than the trees and the stars you have a right to be here.

Whether not it is clear you know the universe is unfolding as it should, therefore be at peace with God whatever you conceive him to be at whatever your labours and aspirations in the noisy confusion of life keep peace with your soul with all its sham drudgery and broken dreams, it is still a beautiful world.

Be careful, strive to be happy

May God be with you always.

Success

Success is awarded those
who dream of endless possibilities
who, through determination
        and perseverance,
continue climbing mountains
and following rainbows

The struggles which we endure
        the battles in which we engage
        the conflicts which we encounter
help us to gain
        a greater perspective of life
it is the benefit of these experiences
        that give our lives meaning

- Mychal Wynn

Other Titles by Kris Patterson

This Was Then...
With Old Ike

A Collection of
excerpts from Ike's
"This Was Then..."
column

Edited
& compiled by
Kris Patterson

This Was Then...
With Old Ike
Volume 2

Another Collection of
excerpts from Ike's
"This Was Then..."
column

Edited
& compiled by
Kris Patterson

I Will Always Love You Ella

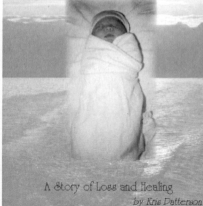

A Story of Loss and Healing
by Kris Patterson

Kris Patterson

Sales
Success

Diagnosing and Prescribing
Customer Solutions

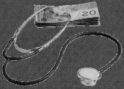

**Delivering Value &
Exceeding Customer Expectations**